Boston Light

Three Centuries of History

Jeremy D'Entremont

Portsmouth, NH

ISBN-13: 978-1530992379
ISBN-10: 1530992370

To the keepers,

from George to Sally

In gratitude for 300 years of dedication.

CONTENTS

INTRODUCTION

Boston Light was my first lighthouse love. I was living in Winthrop, Massachusetts—a peninsula jutting into Boston Harbor—in the 1980s. Inspired by the writings of the popular historian Edward Rowe Snow (1902-1982), I became involved with the Friends of the Boston Harbor Islands. My love for the islands led to an active role in public tours at Boston Light, and it didn't take long to fall deeply in love with Little Brewster Island's beauty and history. The spark that was ignited led me to a career as a writer, tour guide, and photographer specializing in lighthouses.

I'll start by thanking the people who helped strike that spark back in the '80s, particularly Dolly Bicknell (Edward Rowe Snow's daughter), a great friend and lighthouse preservationist in her own right. Suzanne Gall Marsh, founder of Friends of the Boston Harbor Islands, generously provided opportunities for my lighthouse obsession to flourish. Some of the other friends from that era are gone now but live on in happy memories—John Forbes, Skip Empey, and Joe Kolb among them. Many thanks to Willie Emerson and all the Norwoods for sharing their wonderful stories and photos. I also want to acknowledge the late Maurice Babcock Jr. and Harold Jennings, who couldn't have been more helpful when I approached them back in the '80s and '90s. My thanks, also, to Diana Cappiello, descendant of the Babcocks, and Jennifer Fitzpatrick, descendant of Keeper Ted Haskins. I truly appreciate the input of Jill Fredey Doering, daughter of Coast Guard keeper Richard Fredey.

Thanks also to Dennis Dever and all the other Coast Guard keepers who have shared their thoughts. And, of course, I want to express my utmost gratitude to Sally Snowman, America's only official lighthouse keeper, for her generosity, openness, and hospitality.

Of my many research sources, I particularly want to thank the U.S. Coast Guard Historian's Office, the National Archives, the Library of Congress, the American Lighthouse Foundation, the U.S. Lighthouse Society, the Massachusetts Historical Commission, the Friends of the Boston Harbor Islands, the National Park Service, and J. Candace Clifford. Finally, my thanks as always to my wife Charlotte for her help and patience, and to my brother Jim for a lifetime of inspiration, guidance, and support.

In the late 1980s, around the same time I was helping to give tours at Boston Light, I interviewed Ken Black, the man who was known as "Mr. Lighthouse," who would go on to found the Maine Lighthouse Museum. Black described Boston Light: "It's perfect, really. It's what a lighthouse should be." That pretty much sums it up.

Jeremy D'Entremont
Portsmouth, NH
May 2016

1 BEFORE THE LIGHTHOUSE

Boston Light, aptly dubbed the "ideal American lighthouse" by the historian Edward Rowe Snow, holds a place of honor among our nation's beacons. This was the first light station established on the North American continent, and the last in the United States to be automated. It's also our only light station that still retains an official keeper. Seasonal public tours provide the public with the opportunity to experience this cultural treasure up close, and few attractions in New England can approach the thrilling panorama of the harbor and city seen from the lighthouse's lantern.

There were simple lighted beacons in the harbor before the first lighthouse. The primary function of the early beacons was not navigational, but rather to warn of approaching enemy vessels. It's recorded that there was a beacon on Point Allerton in Hull, on the south side of Boston Harbor, as early as 1673—a simple structure supporting an open iron basket or grate in which "fier-bales of pitch and ocre" were burned.

Fitz-Henry Smith Jr., author of *The Story of Boston Light,* published in 1911, believed there might have been an unlighted day beacon on the island we now know as Little Brewster before the lighthouse was established there.

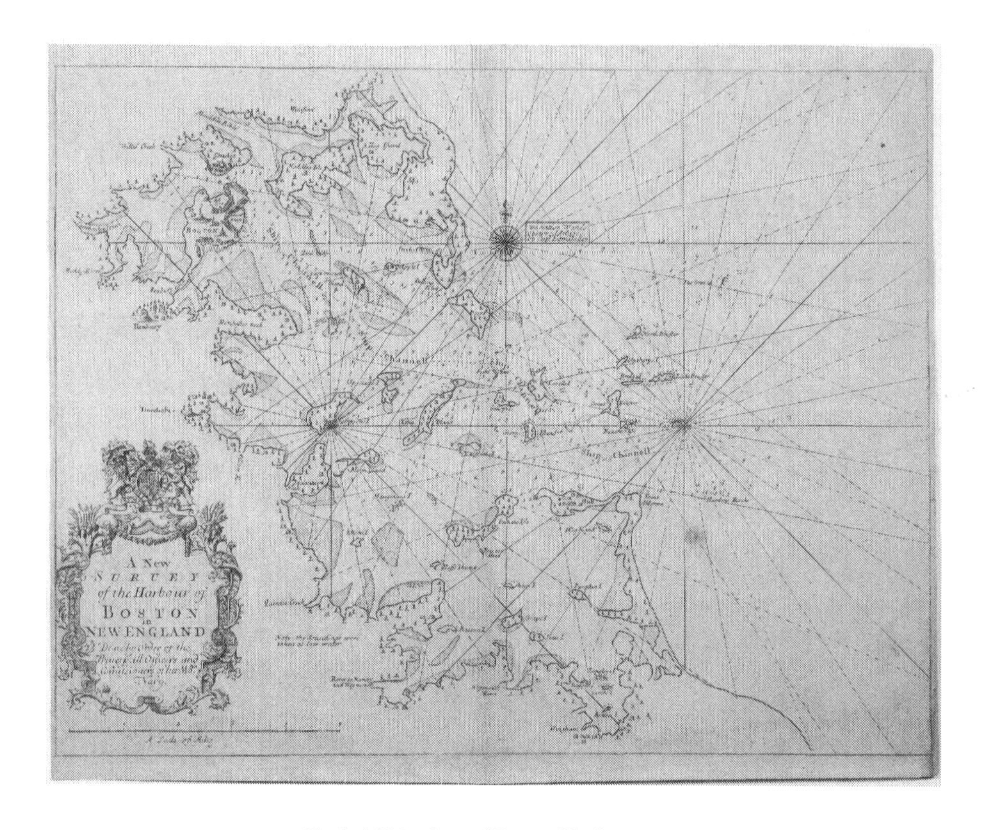

Early 1700s chart of Boston Harbor.

Several islands in Boston's outer harbor are collectively known as the Brewsters, after the Elder Brewster of the Plymouth Colony. Rocky Little Brewster Island—about a mile north of Hull and about eight miles east of Boston—is only about 600 feet long and at most 250 feet wide, its total area just one acre above the mean high water mark. The highest elevation of about 18 feet is at the eastern end of the island, where the lighthouse is located.

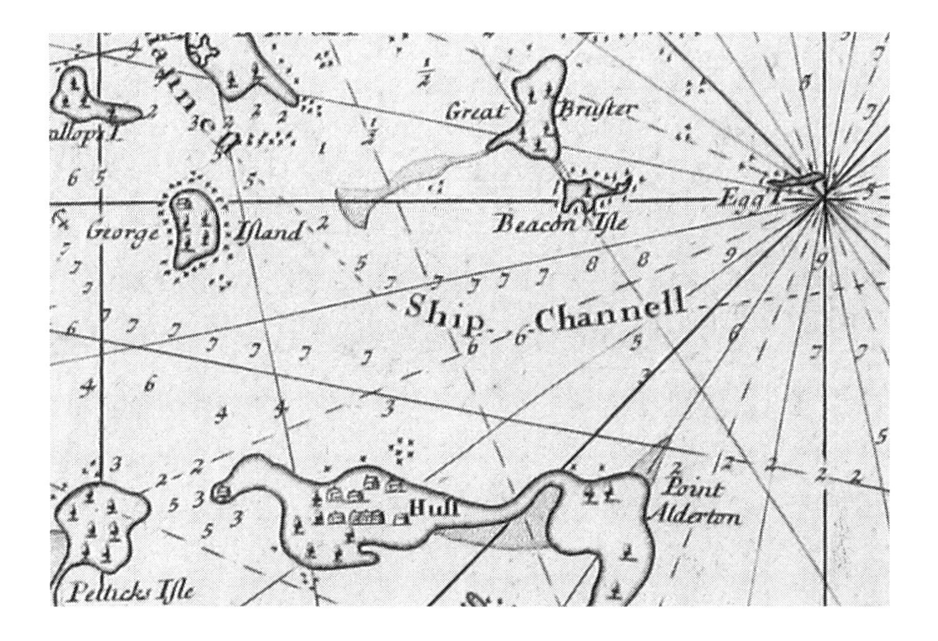

Detail from the early 1700s chart.

Boston's deep and spacious harbor led it to become the commercial center of America in colonial days. At that time all large vessels had to enter the harbor between the Brewster Islands and Point Allerton in the town of Hull.

Clough's *New England Almanac* of 1701 hinted at the need for a lighthouse at the entrance to the harbor. Early in 1713 a prominent Boston merchant and selectman named John George, representing the business community of the city, submitted to the General Court:

> *Proposing the erecting of a Light Hous & Lanthorn on some Head Land at the Entrance to the Harbour of Boston for the Direction of Ships & Vessels in the Night Time bound into the said Harbour.*

John George had also been one of the backers of the building of Boston's half-mile Long Wharf. He didn't live to see the lighthouse established, as he died in November 1714. His widow later married the Reverend Cotton Mather.

A committee headed by Lieutenant Governor William Tailer planned for the lighthouse. After visiting several of the harbor islands and conferring with the area's most experienced shipmasters, Tailer reported that the best site for the lighthouse was "the Southernmost Part of the Great Brewster called Beacon Island." Beacon Island, now known as Little Brewster, is attached to Great Brewster by a sand bar.

After some wrangling on the details, on July 23, 1715, the General Court of Massachusetts passed the Boston Light Bill, the first act passed by any legislative body in North America for the building of a lighthouse. It should be noted that a wooden lighthouse was built at Fort Santo Antônio da Barra in Brazil in 1696; thus, Boston Light was not the first lighthouse in the Western Hemisphere. This was, however, very early in the world's lighthouse history; the famous lighthouse on the Eddystone Rocks in England had been established only 17 years earlier.

The Boston Light Bill read, in part:

Whereas the want of a lighthouse erected at the entrance to the harbor of Boston hath been a great discouragement to navigation by the loss of the lives and estates of several of his majesty's subjects; for prevention thereof—Be it enacted . . . that there be a lighthouse erected at the charge of the Province, on the southernmost part of the Great Brewster, called Beacon Island, to be kept lighted from sun setting to sun rising. . . .

And be it further enacted . . . that the person who shall be appointed from Time to Time by the General Court of the Assembly to be Keeper of the said Light-House, shall carefully and diligently attend his Duty at all Times in kindling the lights from sun-setting to sun-rising, and placing them so as they may be most seen by Vessels coming in or going out . . .

The Brewsters are close to the Point Allerton section of the town of Hull, southeast of Boston. The proprietors of the town of Hull voted unanimously to grant the "Beacken Island" to the province "for the use of a light house forever."

The first lighthouse was financed by a tax of a penny a ton on all vessels coming into the harbor, and the same amount for vessels leaving the harbor. Smaller coasting vessels paid only two shillings as they left the harbor. Fishing vessels and small vessels transporting lumber and other building materials locally were taxed five shillings yearly.

2 THE FIRST TOWER (1716)

A stone tower was built under the direction of Mr. William Payne and Captain Zachariah Tuthill at a cost of 2,385 pounds, 17 shillings, and 8 ½ pence. The exact dimensions aren't known, but it's believed the tower was at least 50 feet tall. It had a wooden lantern with panes of American glass, which was inferior to the French glass of the day.

1729 engraving by William Burgis, with a British sloop in the foreground.

The first keeper, 43-year-old George Worthylake, lighted the lighthouse on Friday, September 14, 1716. The *Boston News Letter* reported a few days later:

> *The said Light House has been built; and on Fryday last the 14th Current the Light was kindled, which will be very useful for all Vessels going out and coming in to the Harbour of Boston, or any other Harbours in the Massachusetts Bay, for which all Masters shall pay to the Receiver of Impost* . . .

No description of the original lighting apparatus survives, but Arnold Burges Johnson wrote in his book *The Modern Light-House Service* that it was "first lighted by tallow candles." The keeper was supplied with "Oyl Week and Candles" in November 1716; it's possible that the lantern originally held both candles and oil lamps. Fish oil was a common illuminant used in early American lighthouse lamps. Whale oil was used from around 1812 to the late 1860s, when it was replaced by lard oil. From the late 1870s to the era of electrification, the primary fuel was kerosene.

Worthylake, who was brought up on Georges Island (previously known as Pemberton Island) in Boston Harbor, moved to the light station with his wife, Ann, and their daughters, Ruth and Ann. Two slaves named Shadwell and Dina also lived with the Worthylakes, and also a servant named George Cutler. Worthylake also maintained a farm on Lovells Island, closer to Boston.

Worthylake was paid £50 a year, which was raised to £70 in

1717. He made additional money as a harbor pilot for incoming vessels, and he also kept a flock of sheep on Great Brewster Island. Fifty-nine of his sheep were caught on the long sand spit off Great Brewster during a 1717 storm, and they drowned when the tide came in.

In early November 1718, Worthylake went to Boston with his wife, their 15-year-old daughter Ruth, and George Cutler. They reportedly attended church in Boston on Sunday, November 2. Some sources indicate that Worthylake also picked up his pay during the visit to the city; in any case, they left to return to Boston Light on Monday morning, November 3.

On their way back the group stopped at Lovells Island, where the Worthylakes and Cutler boarded a sloop heading for Boston Light. A friend, John Edge, accompanied them. Witnesses later said that the party were seen to eat and drink "very friendly" while aboard the sloop, "tho not to excess."

The sloop anchored near Little Brewster Island a few minutes past noon, and Shadwell paddled out in a canoe to transfer the party to the island. Young Ann Worthylake and a friend, Mary Thompson, watched from shore.

Suddenly, the two girls on shore saw "Worthylake, his wife & others swimming or floating on the water, with their boat Oversett." The canoe—possibly overloaded—had capsized, and all six people drowned.

The *Boston News Letter* reported:

On Monday last the 3d Currant an awful Lamentable Providence fell out here. Mr. George Worthylake (Master of the Lighthouse . . . at the Entrance of the Harbour of Boston), Anne his wife, Ruth their daughter, George Cutler, a servant, Shadwell their Negro Slave, and Mr. John Edge a passenger; being on the Lord's Day here all Sermon, and going home in a sloop, drop[ped] Anchor near the landing place, and all got into a little boat or Cannoo, designing to go on to the Shoar, abut by accident it overwhelmed, so that they were Drowned, and all found and interred except George Cutler.

George, Ann, and Ruth Worthylake were buried beneath a triple headstone in Copp's Hill Burying Ground in Boston's North End. The Worthylakes' daughter Ann soon married a stonecutter named John Gaud, who may have carved the triple gravestone at Copp's Hill.

Benjamin Franklin, 12 years old at the time, was urged by his brother to write a poem based on the disaster. The young Franklin wrote a poem called *The Lighthouse Tragedy* and hawked copies on the streets of Boston. Franklin later wrote in his autobiography that the poem was "wretched stuff," although it "sold prodigiously."

Robert Saunders, a former sloop captain, became Boston Light's second keeper on a temporary basis, until a new permanent keeper could be chosen.

The triple gravestone of George, Ann, and Ruth Worthylake in Boston.

Saunders apparently drowned only a few days after arriving on the island. Few details of the incident survive, but a November 24, 1718, item in the *Boston News Letter* tells us the following:

> *Capt. Saunders with Messieurs Braddock and Chamberlain went to the Light-House . . . and espying a Ship coming in from the Sea . . . they concluded to go on Board, which accordingly they did, and in their return they were overset by . . . Wind and drowned except Chamberlain.*

John Hayes, an experienced seaman described as an "able-bodied and discreet person," became the next keeper. His salary was at first only £50 yearly, but it was raised to £85 by 1720.

In 1719, Hayes asked for a gallery, or balcony, to be installed around the tower's lantern room so that he could clean the glass of ice and snow. He also noted the need for some kind of fog signal, asking that "a great Gun may be placed on the Said Island to answer Ships in a Fogg."

A cannon, America's first fog signal, was placed on the island in 1719. Passing ships would fire their cannons when passing nearby in times of fog, and the keeper would reply with a blast from the light station. Around this time the keeper was also required to signal if enemy vessels were approaching by raising and lowering a flag "so many Times as there are Ships approaching."

The fog cannon, now on display in the entryway to the tower.

The cannon, cast in 1700 and possibly relocated from Long Island in the inner harbor, served on Little Brewster Island for 132 years. In 1962, the cannon was moved to the Coast Guard Academy in New London, Connecticut, where it was placed in a position facing the Thames River. In 1993 it was returned by helicopter to Little Brewster, and the venerable fog cannon sits today on a new carriage inside the entryway to the lighthouse tower.

A fire broke out in the lighthouse's lantern room during the evening of January 13, 1720, caused by "the lamps dropping on ye wooden benches and snuff falling off and setting fire," according to Hayes. Hayes's wife roused the keeper around 8:00 p.m. and informed him of the fire, and Hayes quickly ran up the stairs of the tower with two pails of water. He later reported that the "fire was too violent to be subdued," but he "saved many things belonging to the Light House."

The damage was severe; in fact, the *Boston News Letter* reported that the lighthouse had "burnt down." It cost around £400 to repair the damage. The lighthouse was reported to be in operation again by February 17. Hayes's salary was withheld until he was absolved of the blame.

In 1722, during a smallpox epidemic in the area, Hayes was charged with the added duty of informing incoming vessels of the situation and requiring them to be quarantined. He complained of the extra work and was given an extra £20 for his trouble.

A storm in February 1723 brought record high tides to the area that damaged the lighthouse and the island's wharf. A committee examined the lighthouse after the great storm and found several cracks in the stone, particularly in the lighthouse's interior. It wasn't clear if the cracks were caused by the storm or by the earlier fire. The tower was repointed and encased in "Good oak Plank" in the mid-1730s, and 12 iron hoops were added around the exterior for added strength.

In October 1727, a sloop from North Carolina, bound for Boston, went aground near the lighthouse as a storm was building. The captain, John Bangs, sent a man to the lighthouse, where he implored the keeper to come with his boat to help get the sloop back into deeper water. Hayes ultimately towed the sloop to Boston, where the winds and seas drove it against the shore causing considerable damage. Hayes asked for reimbursement for damages to his boat, but the incident brought on accusations that the keeper was "old and crazy" and unfit for service.

A curious advertisement in a newspaper called the *Weekly Rehearsal*, dated September 3, 1733, informs us that Hayes had an "English manservant" named John Elwood with him on the island. It seems Elwood had run away, and Hayes wanted him back. Elwood was described as a "short, well set fellow with a broad red face," and was last seen wearing a "striped homespun jacket" and "cinnamon-coloured plush breeches." Hayes offered a reward of 40 shillings for the return of his servant.

John Hayes retired "on account of age and infirmities" in 1733. Robert Ball, an Englishman whose stay of about 40 years would be the longest stint of any keeper in the station's history, succeeded him. On the day after Hayes resigned, Ball married Martha King of Charlestown. Ball was assisted on the island by a slave known as Samson, who died in 1762 and was buried on Rainsford Island in the harbor.

1733 illustration from the New England Coasting Pilot.

The *Boston Gazette* of March 24, 1735, reported an incident that echoed the 1718 Worthylake and Saunders tragedies. A sudden gust of wind had upset the lighthouse boat. Three persons were "providentially saved," but a man named John Kerigan drowned in the accident.

A day of "Showers of Rain, and hard Gusts of Wind, attended with Severe Thunder and Lightning" did much damage in the Boston area in May 1738, according to the *New England Weekly Journal.* Several boats had their sails split by the wind, and hailstones "as big as midling Bullets" broke the windows of the lighthouse "to pieces."

The keeper still doubled as a harbor pilot during Ball's stay. Ball complained in 1739 that other enterprising individuals were taking many of the piloting jobs, which he felt rightfully belonged to him. The court pronounced Ball the "established pilot" for the harbor and announced that anyone else painting his boat to resemble Ball's would be fined five pounds, to be paid to Ball. Ball seems to have made out well financially; he eventually owned three of the harbor islands—Outer Brewster, Calf Island, and Green Island.

The early keepers were given a tavern license, as it was apparently expected that they would entertain visitors on the island. Ball appears to have been a hospitable host, judging by the account of a Boston merchant named John Fayerweather. In June 1746 he invoiced the Town of Boston for the sum of 50 shillings, repaying him for "cash paid ye Light-House tavern for meetings held there with ye Committee to measure ye rocks from ye lower middle ground," plus a smaller sum "for drink for the boat's crew in April."

Another bad fire gutted the lighthouse in 1751. The tower was sheathed in wood by this time, which contributed to the quick spread of the fire. For a time after this the light was shown from a lantern on a 40-foot spar. After repairs totaling £1,170, including the replacement of the original wooden lantern with one made of iron (with a copper roof), a higher duty was imposed on local shipping.

The lighthouse was struck by lightning on several occasions in its early history, including an instance in June 1754 when lightning "tore off shingles from several places on the outside." The installation of a lightning rod was delayed because of the objections of some "godly men" who thought it "vanity and irreligion for the arm of flesh to presume to avert the stroke of heaven," according to a 1789 article. Practicality eventually won out and a lightning conductor was installed.

More repairs to the lighthouse were in the works when the American Revolution intervened. In July 1775 Boston Harbor and the lighthouse were under the control of the British. On July 20, American troops under Maj. Joseph Vose landed at the lighthouse and took lamps, oil, and some gunpowder and burned the wooden parts of the tower. After leaving the island they had to outrun an armed British schooner, and two Americans were wounded. An eyewitness described "the flames of the lighthouse ascending up to Heaven, like grateful incense, and the ships wasting their powder."

As the British worked to repair the tower, 300 American soldiers under Maj. Benjamin Tupper landed at the island on July 31. They easily defeated the British guard and again burned the lighthouse. As they tried to leave, they found their boats stranded, for the tide had gone out. This gave British vessels time to reach the scene.

The Americans finally managed to launch their boats as the British fired on them. American troops at Nantasket in Hull helped by firing a cannon, landing a direct hit on one of the British vessels. This turned the tide of battle and the Americans escaped with only one soldier having been killed. Gen. George Washington praised the men:

> *The General thanks Major Tupper and the Officers and Soldiers under his Command, for their gallant and soldierlike behaviour in possessing themselves of the enemy's post at the Light House, and for the Number of Prisoners they took there, and doubts not, but the Continental Army, will be as famous for their mercy as for their valour.*

A wounded British prisoner, left by Major Tupper at Hull, died a short time later and was buried in the garden of Royal Navy Lieutenant William Haswell, who was under house arrest. The prisoner's story was later woven into a 1792 novel, *Rebecca*, written by Haswell's daughter, Susanna Rowson. Rowson also wrote the book *Charlotte Temple*, which was the best-selling American novel before *Uncle Tom's Cabin.*

At the end of their occupation of Boston Harbor during the war, the British lingered in the harbor for some months. Nathaniel Bradstreet Shurtleff described what happened in June 1776 in his book *A Topographical and Historical Description of Boston*:

> *On the thirteenth of June, 1776, nearly three months after the British were obliged to take refuge on board their vessels, the Continentals began to bring their guns to bear on their enemy, and on the fourteenth, Mr. Ezekiel Price narrates, . . . "the cannon began from Long Island to play upon the shipping which obliged them to weigh their anchors, and make the best of their way out of their harbor. As they passed Nantasket and the*

Lighthouse, our artillery gave them some shot from Nantasket Hill. The enemy sent their boats on shore at the Light-House Island, and brought from thence a party, there placed, of Regulars; after which they destroyed the Light-House, and then the whole fleet made all the sail they could, and went to sea, steering their course eastward." The commander of the ship, the Renown, *of fifty guns, Captain Bangs, after taking his men from the island, left a quantity of gunpowder so arranged that it took fire in about an hour afterward, and blew up the brick* [sic] *tower.*

The blast destroyed the tower; the remains of the metal lantern were reportedly used to make ladles for American cannons. It has sometimes been claimed that part of the original tower was incorporated into the second one. While there is no evidence to support this assertion, it certainly seems feasible that some of the rubblestone from the old tower could have been used.

C. early 1780s, from a painting by Capt. Matthew Parke.

This image apparently depicts the original tower before its 1776 destruction.

According to some sources, Keeper Robert Ball (whose nephew, William Minns, had served as keeper from some time in 1774 until July 1775) sailed away with the British fleet to Halifax in 1776, never to be seen in Boston Harbor again. But according to an October 1895 article in *New England Magazine,* written by G. F. Candage after the destruction of the lighthouse in June 1776, Ball was certified by the Boston Committee of Correspondence as a person "friendly to the Rights and Liberties of Americans." His son Robert, a sea captain, owned several Boston Harbor islands, which he willed to his son and daughter in the late 1700s.

More action was seen near the island in the summer of 1780 when the 50-gun British ship *Sagittaire* attacked a convoy coming from Newport, Rhode Island. The British captured a French frigate in the convoy and the French sailors who died in the battle were thrown into the waters of the outer harbor.

With no navigational aid at the entrance to the harbor, an unlighted beacon was placed at the end of the spit extending from Great Brewster in 1780.

3 THE SECOND TOWER AND LIFE ON THE ISLAND 1783 TO 1862

Governor John Hancock of Massachusetts recommended the rebuilding of the lighthouse in November 1780, pointing out that "without a lighthouse to guide shipping to Boston, the people could not expect a return to the days of good shipping."

In spite of Hancock's pleas, no immediate action was taken. Finally, in June 1783 a committee of the Boston Marine Society addressed the lack of a lighthouse. The commissary general of Massachusetts, Richard Devens, was authorized to build a new lighthouse on the original site.

The new 60-foot (75 feet to the top of the octagonal lantern), conical rubblestone tower was designed to be "nearly of the same dimensions of the former lighthouse." The cost of construction was $19,881.44. The tower was 45 feet in circumference at the base, rising to a lantern that was 25 feet in circumference. The walls were 7.5 feet thick at the base and 2.5 feet thick at the top.

Thomas Knox was the first post-Revolution keeper. His parents,

Adam and Martha, lived with him on the island. Martha Knox died in January 1790, and Adam died in December of the same year. Adam Knox owned Nix's Mate Island in the harbor, and Thomas inherited ownership when his father died.

Knox was keeper for 27 years, also serving as a harbor pilot. Two of his brothers were also harbor pilots. In an article published in 1789, Knox described the lighting apparatus as four lamps, each holding a gallon of oil, and each having four lights. The lamps were divided into four sections that each operated independently. There were complaints that the light was too dim when seen from the sea, and the lamps produced a great deal of smoke.

The *Massachusetts Magazine* of February 1789 published detailed sailing directions into Boston Harbor, written by Thomas Knox in his role as the "branch pilot" for the Port of Boston. He included the following advice, possibly in defense of his own safety: "If the weather is bad you cannot get a Pilot from the Light House."

The light station was ceded to the federal government on June 10, 1790, a year after lighthouses had been put under the management of the U.S Treasury Department. With the change, Knox lost his title as Boston's official "branch pilot." Governor Hancock assigned that designation to another man, but Knox continued to work as a pilot. In 1794 Knox's yearly salary as keeper was set by the federal government at $266.67, which was raised to $333.33 in 1796.

Knox apparently requested a new boat in 1796. Tench Coxe, commissioner of Revenue and supervisor of federal lighthouse operations at the time, wrote the following in a letter to General Benjamin Lincoln—customs collector for Boston and local lighthouse superintendent—on June 9, 1796:

> *It is not perceived that there can be any public uses for a boat at the Boston Light House. The keeper has no public calls from the Islands. If he had there are numerous opportunities of going up to the Town in bay craft pilot boats . . . As far as the matter is understood at present it is conceived that the expence of a boat ought not to be incurred.*

In June 1809 the local lighthouse superintendent, Henry Dearborn, found three perpendicular cracks in the tower, extending for almost its entire height. Six iron hoops were added around the tower for extra support. One band was removed in the early twentieth century; five aluminum bands are in place today.

Winslow Lewis, a member of the Boston Marine Society, began experiments with lighthouse illumination around 1807. He patented his system of Argand-type lamps (more efficient and less smoky than the old lamps) paired with parabolic reflectors in 1810. He first demonstrated his system in the cupola of the State House in Boston.

Lewis's system was subsequently installed at Boston Light in May 1810. Six whale oil–fueled lamps were installed in two parallel rows, about 15 inches apart. A parabolic reflector was placed behind each lamp. An observer on a vessel about nine miles from both

Boston Light and the light station at Baker's Island, near Salem, reported:

> *The difference in the brightness of these and the Light at Baker's island was as great as would appear between a well trimmed Argand lamp and a common Candle. . . . At 11 o'clock these were extinguished and the common lamps relighted—the effect produced by the change from light to comparative darkness was more striking than the first. We now stood towards the Lighthouse. At 12 o'clock the Argand Lamps were again lighted . . . When within two and an half leagues their power was so great as to throw a strong Shadow on the deck of the Vessel.*

The lighthouse had exhibited a fixed white light, but in 1811 machinery was installed that enabled the light to revolve. The *American Coast Pilot* around this time described a revolving light that appeared at full brilliancy for 40 seconds, and then was obscured for 20 seconds. This, in theory, made it easier for mariners to differentiate Boston Light from the new light established at Scituate a few miles down the coast. In reality, many wrecks resulted from confusion between the lights.

The Boston Marine Society urged the adoption of Lewis's apparatus in all American lighthouses, and he was subsequently awarded a contract for that purpose. This system remained in use in the United States into the 1850s, long after much of the rest of the world had adopted the use of the more efficient Fresnel lens invented in France in 1822.

Jonathan H. Bruce followed Knox as keeper in 1811; his appointment was recommended by the Boston Marine Society. Bruce served as a harbor pilot, as his son, also named Jonathan, did in later years. Surviving correspondence indicates that Knox remained living in a dwelling on the island for some time after Bruce became keeper.

Details are sketchy, but the light was apparently extinguished during the War of 1812, as there is a record of its relighting in 1814. On June 1, 1813, the British ship *Shannon* battled the American frigate *Chesapeake*. It's been claimed that Bruce and his wife, Mary, watched the battle from the island. If so, it was a distant view, as the ships were about 12 miles away, possibly seen with the use of a telescope from the top of the lighthouse. The *Chesapeake* was swiftly defeated in about 15 minutes, but not before the mortally wounded Capt. James Lawrence uttered the immortal words "Don't give up the ship!"

Jonathan Bruce left Boston Light in 1833 and moved to Rainsford Island in Boston Harbor. Lt. Edward W. Carpender inspected the station in 1838, while David Tower was the keeper. Carpender described the lighting apparatus as 14 lamps and parabolic reflectors—varying from 13 1/2 to 16 inches in diameter—arranged on opposite sides of an oblong frame or chandelier. The entire apparatus revolved, completing a revolution every three and one-half minutes. Keeper Tower complained that the lantern leaked, which sometimes caused the rotating mechanism to stop and forced him to turn the apparatus by hand.

1839 illustration from Paris

Like his predecessors, Tower doubled as a harbor pilot. Carpender noted that this practice took Tower away from the lighthouse frequently at night, and he recommended that keepers be forbidden by law to take on any pursuits that removed them from their station during the hours that they should be concerned, above all, with the lighting of the lamps.

Apparently owing in large part to recommendations made by Carpender, Winslow Lewis installed a new lantern in 1839, along with new 21-inch reflectors from England. The *Portsmouth Journal of*

Literature and Politics sang the praises of the improved light:

> *The light is of great brilliancy—and burst upon the sight at the distance of twenty miles, with surprising effect, insomuch that in some instances the wondering mariner has hardly dared to trust to the evidence of his senses—but has feared that he was deceived by some brilliant pyrotechnical experiments on shore, until the regularity of the [r]evolutions, and the uniformity of the flashes, convinced him that it could be no other than Boston Light, astonishingly improved.*

The engineer I. W. P. Lewis, Winslow Lewis's nephew, visited Boston Light for his important 1843 report to Congress. The keeper's house and boathouse were in good order, and the light was a good one that could be seen "in clear weather 13 ¾ miles with perfect distinctness." But Lewis's report found much wrong with the tower:

> *Tower of rubble masonry, sixty-six feet high, laid up in lime mortar; base resting on solid rock; soapstone roof, loose and leaky, disjointed; walls seriously injured by the effects of frost The water and spray is driven up in storms under the eaves of the soapstone deck, percolates downward through the interstices of the masonry, freezes in winter, throws out the pointing, and disturbs the bond of the stone work. The tower is hooped outside with heavy bands of wrought iron, to prevent its walls from bulging out and falling to pieces. The staircase and landing are of wood, and all so rotten as to be unsafe of ascent. The window frames are of iron, except the upper one, which*

is wood, and rotten. The entire structure requires a very complete repair.

An inspection by the local superintendent in 1843 called the station "one of the very best on the coast," but agreed with Lewis on the need for a new deck below the lantern.

David Tower died in 1844 after a brief illness. That same year a new cast-iron spiral stairway with a wrought-iron railing was installed; the stairway is still in use today. Iron doors and window frames were also installed. Most of the additions made at that time remain in place today.

Joshua Snow followed Tower as keeper. Around this time an unusual enterprise was in operation on Little Brewster Island—a "Spanish cigar factory," staffed by young girls from Boston. The cigars the girls made were labeled as "Cuban" and were sold to unsuspecting locals. The authorities soon broke up the illegal business. Some sources place the cigar factory during the tenure of the next keeper, but it seems more likely that it operated during Snow's stay. Snow left in December 1844, apparently dismissed after only a few months on the island.

Tobias Cook of Cohasset, Massachusetts, was the next keeper, staying until 1849. Following Cook was William Long of Charlestown, Massachusetts. An 1851 inspection was somewhat critical of Long, noting that he didn't light up at sunset or put out the light precisely at sunrise. The tower was in need of whitewashing, and the copper lightning conductors were broken and neglected by the keeper.

In *Famous Lighthouses of New England,* the historian Edward Rowe Snow included some passages from the 1849–51 diary of Keeper Long's daughter, Lucy:

Monday. October 29—Pleasant weather, in the forenoon I went in the cutter's boat to carry Antoinette to the Pilot Boat "Hornet." In the afternoon I went over to the island, on returning saw the body of a man on the bar, supposedly washed from the wreck of the vessel, lost on Minot's Ledge.

Mon. Dec. 31—A snowstorm in the morning. George came over to wind up the clock, and I cleaned the light, at night I light the light.

Monday, Aug. 26—Pleasant weather, this morning Albert came down in his boat.

"Albert" was Albert Small, a harbor pilot. Despite much competition, Small won the hand of Lucy Maria Long in marriage. His proposal came at the top of the lighthouse, and the two were wed in 1853.

A 1,375-pound fog bell, operated by clockwork machinery, replaced the old fog cannon in 1851. The bell was struck every 47 seconds in times of poor visibility, and it operated for six hours on a single winding.

Zebedee Small was keeper from 1851 to 1853, followed by Hugh Douglass (1853–56). During Douglass's stay, the rotation of the lens was speeded up to a revolution every one and one-half minute.

A Gloucester native, Moses Barrett, saw much change during his time as keeper (1856–62). The Lighthouse Board suggested in 1857 that the tower be rebuilt at a cost of $71,000, but improvements were made instead. In 1859 the tower was raised to its present height of 89 feet and a new lantern was installed along with a 12-sided, second-order Fresnel lens manufactured by L. Sautter in Paris.

Looking into the lens from below.

The giant lens—about 11 feet tall and 15 feet in circumference—rotated by means of a clockwork mechanism that required frequent winding. A single lamp inside the new lens replaced the system of multiple lamps, and round "bull'seye" panels on the lens produced a flash each time they passed in front of the light source. The lens went into operation on December 20, 1859.

In the same year the tower was lined with brick, a spacious brick entryway was added to the tower, and a new duplex keeper's house was built. Beginning in 1861, Boston Light was assigned a keeper and two assistants.

Barrett witnessed one of Boston Harbor's worst tragedies on November 8, 1861, when the 991-ton ship *Maritana* ran into Shag Rocks in the outer harbor—about an eighth of a mile from Boston Light—during a heavy snow squall in the predawn hours. The ship, with 39 people aboard, had been heading for Boston from Liverpool. Around 8:30 a.m. the ship broke in two, and Captain George Williams was killed.

Barrett signaled the town of Hull, and a pilot boat soon sent a dory to Shag Rocks. A dozen people were rescued, largely through the superhuman efforts of Captain Samuel James of Hull, but 27 died in the wreck. During the following spring, the captain's wife journeyed to Little Brewster Island to receive her husband's watch and other belongings that Barrett had been holding for her.

4 LIFE ON THE ISLAND, 1862 TO 1916

The Civil War had little direct impact on Boston Light, but Charles E. Blair, keeper from 1862 to 1864, witnessed Confederate prisoners being transported to Boston Harbor's Fort Warren, which served as a prison during the war.

The next keeper, Thomas Bates, took over in July 1864 and remained until his death in April 1893. The light station was the scene of many happy gatherings during the Bates era. Frequent sing-alongs took place, with the accompaniment of Assistant Keeper Edward Gorham on accordion. *When the Roll Is Called Up Yonder* and *Crossing the Bar* were special favorites.

In 1868, during a period of improvements at the station, the sloop *Billow*—carrying 80 tons of stone for the protection of the island's piers, became caught between the piers when the tide fell. The ship couldn't be extricated until some time later, when it was towed to Quincy and sold at auction.

On January 31, 1882, Keeper Bates, along with an assistant keeper and a local fisherman, rescued the crew of the sail vessel *Fanny Pike,* which had run into Shag Rocks.

Keeper Thomas Bates, courtesy of Dolly Bicknell.

There were many changes and improvements during Bates' tenure, including a change of the light's fuel from lard oil to kerosene in 1883. A brick cistern was added in the following year in a building near the tower. The cistern held 21,800 gallons of rainwater for the keepers and their families.

A second keeper's house was added in 1885, located at the opposite end of the island from the lighthouse. Two houses had become a necessity with three keepers and their families living on the island. The 1859 duplex house near the lighthouse became the home for the two assistant keepers and their families, while the smaller 1885 served as the home for the principal keeper and his family.

A Daboll compressed-air fog trumpet replaced the bell in 1872. It remained in use until 1887, when a steam-driven siren replaced it. For a number of years, a railway system was used to get shipments of coal from the pier to the fog signal building. In the 1930s, 21 tons of coal was delivered to the station every fall.

In the late nineteenth century students from the Massachusetts Institute of Technology conducted experiments with fog signals at Boston Light, trying to perfect a signal that would penetrate the so-called ghost walk, an area about six miles east of the lighthouse where no sound could penetrate. Despite the students' best efforts, even the largest horn could not penetrate the ghost walk.

When Thomas Bates died at Massachusetts General Hospital on April 6, 1893, at the age of 62, the *Boston Globe* reported that the cause of death was "sarcoma of the stomach," which was said to have been caused by his cramped quarters at the lighthouse.

Alfred M. Horte had a brief stay as keeper and was succeeded by Henry L. Pingree, who was keeper from 1894 to 1909. Pingree's son, Wesley, who was an assistant keeper at

Deer Island Light in Boston Harbor, married Horte's sister, Josephine.

Fog signal engine at Boston Light, late 1800s. From the New York Public Library.

An auxiliary light was added to the station in 1890—a fixed white light was exhibited from a small wooden building. The light was designed to help mariners avoid dangerous Hardings Ledge. If they strayed too far from the channel to either side, they would see a red light. A short time later, in 1891-92, a new chariot wheel assembly for the rotation of the Fresnel lens was created in a Boston machine shop and installed in the lighthouse.

Late nineteenth century view (U.S. Coast Guard)

Wesley Pingree later served for a time as an assistant to his father at Boston Light. Edward Rowe Snow tells us that on one occasion, Wesley Pingree was shocked to see the steamer *Portland* in the confined area between Shag Rocks and Outer Brewster Island. The vessel was backed out without incident, but it later sank in a snowstorm in November 1898 with the loss of many lives.

A February 1895 article in the *Boston Globe* described a voyage aboard a tugboat to deliver newspapers to lighthouses in the Boston area. The scene at Boston Light was described:

Oil storage room inside the entryway to the tower, late 1800s. From the New York Public Library.

Keeper H. L. Pingree came down from his house and his face shown with delight as he saw the roll of Globes and was told that the tug had come down for the sole purpose of bringing them.

"Thank the Globe people heartily for me," he exclaimed. "We have had no mail, no newspapers, nor no tidings from the outside world for 14 days, and that's a long time."

"Here comes my son, who is my first assistant, and Gershom Freeman, the second assistant. They have just been trying to get over to Fort Warren for the mail, but the ice drove them back. I

was feeling pretty blue at the prospect of another day's delay, you may believe. I have letters, too, I want to send."

He was assured that his mail would be taken safely to Boston and the cover was soon torn from the precious newspapers, his son hurrying up to join in the mental treat.

Mr. Pingree said the past week had been a wild one at the light, although he and his family had not suffered. The flying spray went completely over the houses and froze hard, while even the lighthouse itself was covered for a long distance up.

Circa 1897 (U.S. Coast Guard)

Pingree was involved in the rescue of five men on March 19, 1906. A three-masted schooner, the *C. C. Lane* of New Haven, carrying a cargo of clay, was drifting in the gale without a compass or a lifeboat. As the weather cleared around midnight, Pingree spotted the schooner on the ledges near the lighthouse. With his two assistants, Charles W. Jordan and Henry C. Towle, Pingree went out in a boat and boarded the *Lane*, and took the crewmen back to the safety of the light station. When he reached them, the men had been huddled in the lee of the bowsprit on the sinking vessel for about three hours. All five were on a tug bound for Boston on the next day.

The storm saw scores of wrecks around New England, with several lives lost. Jordan and Towle were later awarded silver lifesaving medals for their bravery.

Just two months later, on May 20, 1906, First Assistant Keeper Charles W. Jordan was credited with saving the lives of two brothers from South Boston. Early in the morning, Jordan spotted Bartley Foley, 39, and John Foley, 28, fighting nasty seas in their dory as a sudden squall struck.

The dory capsized, and when Jordan got to them they were barely staying above the waves and they tried to hang onto the overturned boat. About a half mile from the lighthouse, Jordan was able to haul them one at a time into his boat. The lucky men were taken to Little Brewster Island, where they were given dry clothing, breakfast, and hot coffee. Jordan, 23 years old at the time, said that the Foleys were "exceptionally cool" under the circumstances.

Pingree was principal keeper until 1909. The next keeper, Levi B. Clark, weathered a tremendous blizzard on Christmas Day that year. The five-masted schooner *Davis Palmer*, carrying a cargo of coal, struck Finn's Ledge, north of the Brewster Islands, and sank with all hands in the storm. Some of the wreckage came ashore at Little Brewster Island.

A 1910 newspaper article described the small school that operated on the third floor of the principal keeper's house. Before then, children of the keepers were usually transported by boat to Hull to attend school, but there were many days when rough weather and seas made the trip hazardous. With five children among the keepers' families, a schoolteacher was sent to the island—Mela Hanchard of Hull. Ms. Hanchard lived on the island during the week; she said she was always sorry when Fridays came and she had to leave.

According to the article, a small organ helped with music lessons, and there was a library of about 200 books available for use in the tiny school. When lessons were over, the teacher often went rowing or fishing with the keepers and children. The children's island playmates were also described in the article: a bulldog puppy named Mutt, a tame raccoon named Pete, and multiple cats.

5 LIFE ON THE ISLAND, 1916-1941

Charles Jennings, a Cape Cod native previously stationed at Monomoy Point Light, became keeper in 1916 at a yearly salary of $804. Jennings was on hand, along with First Assistant Keeper Charles A. Lyman, for a celebration of Boston Light's 200th anniversary. A commemorative bronze plaque was unveiled at the lighthouse on the morning of September 25, 1916, with dignitaries arriving aboard the lighthouse tender *Mayflower*. Commissioner of Lighthouses George R. Putnam served as the master of ceremonies. His remarks included the following:

> *The city of Boston was a leader in the development of maritime commerce on the shores of this continent, and this lighthouse is intimately associated with the history of this city and the development of its maritime interests.*

After the ceremony, in the afternoon, another observance was held at Boston's Old State House. The

Secretary of Commerce, William Redfield, was on hand, and Massachusetts Governor Samuel McCall was one of the speakers. A clambake (price, $2.00) in Hull that evening topped off the day's celebrations, with Fitz-Henry Smith Jr., who had written a history of Boston Light, as a featured speaker.

Photo by G. F. Radway, taken on September 14, 1916. Courtesy of Dolly Bicknell.

It was noted during the 200th anniversary celebrations that Little Brewster Island had no American flag. In June 1917, the Boston Chamber of Commerce remedied the situation by presenting a 65-foot steel flagpole and a flag. The dedication ceremony included a U.S. Navy delegation, Chamber officials, and other dignitaries. The flag was raised for the first time by Keeper Jennings and Arthur Small, an assistant keeper.

In his book *A Lighthouse Family,* Charles Jennings' son, Harold, described a celebrated rescue his father performed in 1918:

> *On February 3, 1918, the U.S.S.* Alacrity, *a Coast Guard patrol boat, ran aground in the ice a few yards from the station. The tide was ebbing fast and it wasn't long before the vessel lay over on her side. This made it impossible for the crew to launch their lifeboat. Dad and the assistant keeper saw their plight and began figuring out how to rescue the crew. They reasoned that if they tried to get a dory through the ice cakes, they would be crushed. Dad remembered that in the boathouse there was some gunpowder and firing caps that were used in the old cannon, originally used as a fog signal at the light. The assistant keeper got a coil of rope that could be used. They set the fuse and pushed the gunpowder down the barrel. They made a hard ball in the end of the rope. The remaining coil lay next to the cannon. The fuse was ignited and when the gun fired, the rope followed the ball out to the ship. It was not quite on target so they tried again with no success. Now they had to launch the dory and take a chance that the ice did not close in on them. After a couple of trips, carrying the crew and gear, the rescue was a success. This was the last time the fog cannon was*

fired at Boston Light.

Jennings, who received a commendation from the secretary of Commerce for the rescue of 24 men from the *Alacrity,* moved on to be the keeper of the range lights at Lovell's Island in 1919.

John Lelan Hart was keeper from 1919 to 1926. In 1921 Hart and his assistant, William J. Howard—who later gained fame as a lifesaver at Wing's Neck Light on Cape Cod—were credited with saving the life of the second assistant keeper, whose boat had capsized. Hart was involved in several more rescues during his stay.

Three keepers of Boston Light: Charles Jennings, Maurice Babcock, and John Lelan Hart. Courtesy of Dolly Bicknell.

Maurice Alendo Babcock, formerly at Thacher Island, Bird Island, and Gay Head, was principal keeper from 1926 to 1941. Babcock was born in Campobello, New Brunswick, Canada, in 1888. He and his wife had two sons and two daughters.

Keeper Maurice Babcock and family. Courtesy of John Babcock and Diana Cappiello.

The Babcocks' children boarded in the nearby towns of Winthrop or Hull so they could attend school, and they spent their vacations on Little Brewster. On one occasion Keeper Babcock rowed through dangerous ice floes to Hull to pick up his son Bill during a February vacation. The keeper's wife watched her husband fight off giant ice cakes as he headed for Hull. She lost sight of him for an agonizing two hours. Finally, she caught sight of the returning dory, with her husband rowing and their son fending off the ice.

"After I had given them a good scolding," she later said, "I sat them down to a hot supper and we had a pleasant holiday." Bill Babcock later carried on the family tradition, becoming a keeper at Graves Light in Boston Harbor.

Archford Vernon "Ted" Haskins, like Babcock a native of New Brunswick, Canada, was an assistant keeper for about a decade beginning in 1927. Haskins ultimately served 32 years as a lighthouse keeper, with later stints at Great Point and Sankaty Head on Nantucket and Owls Head in Maine. When he retired, he was one of the last civilian lighthouse keepers in the United States.

Keeper Ted Haskins circa 1945. Courtesy of Marla Rogers and Jennifer Fitzpatrick.

Haskins and his family shared the 1859 duplex house near the lighthouse tower with the family of the other assistant keeper. Haskins' children later recalled that every chore was more difficult at an island light station. When she wanted to wash the family's clothes, Haskins' wife, Betty, had to collect the water a bucket at a time from the basement. The water was heated on a stove overnight, and the clothes were washed using washboard and lye soap.

The Haskins' school aged children spent weekends and vacations on the island, and stayed in a boardinghouse on the mainland during the school week. Transportation was via a small boat called the *Dolittle*—so named because it did little.

Ted Haskins picked up large quantities of food on the mainland when he had the opportunity. Canned food comprised most of the family's diet in winter. "If they had to have corn chowder three nights in a row, that's what they did," Haskins' daughter Marla Haskins Rogers said in an interview many years later.

Ralph Clough Norwood, a Maine native who left a job at a textile mill to join the Lighthouse Service, was an assistant keeper beginning in 1929. In his book *The Romance of Boston* Bay, Edward Rowe Snow called Norwood an "expert oarsman" who thought nothing of a 20 or 30-mile trip by dory along the coast. Lighthouses were in his blood; his grandfather was Albert Norwood, keeper of Wood Island Light in Biddeford, Maine.

Ralph and Josephine Norwood. Courtesy of Willie Emerson.

In the spring of 1932, Josephine Norwood, Ralph's wife, was expecting their seventh child. (She would have nine children by the time she reached 27.) During an early April storm, Josephine believed the birth was imminent and Dr. Walter H. Sturgis was summoned from Hull. Dr. Sturgis said later:

I got the call from Boston Light about 7 that night. We phoned Captain Josephs, who said he would meet us at Pemberton (in Hull) and Sylvia and myself hopped in the Auburn (car) and sped for the point. When we arrived, we could hear the Coast Guard boat turning the point to get on the lee side of the sea wall. We couldn't see them . . . the rain was driving like hell.

Unable to see the boat, Sturgis went to the Coast Guard station where he boarded a dory that took him to the larger boat. It took an hour and a half for the boat to land at the island in heavy seas.

All preparations were made for the birth, but it was a case of false labor. When Sturgis returned to the Coast Guard station, he was surprised to be greeted by a bevy of reporters. As it turned out, Georgia wasn't born until a week later on April 11 in calm weather, but the headlines from the night of the storm forever stamped Georgia as the "Storm Child."

The writer Ruth Carmen based a novel called *Storm Child* on the story. The book, a highly fictionalized version of the Norwoods' story, even included a tidal wave destroying the lighthouse. Georgia and her parents were showered with publicity, and they traveled to New York City to appear on the nationally broadcast *We the People* program.

Hollywood subsequently came calling to make a movie version of *Storm Child,* and five-year-old Georgia was slated to play herself. Described as "smiling and sunny-curled," Georgia was to be the "Bay State's own Shirley Temple."

Ralph Norwood and daughter Georgia in the 1930s. Courtesy of Willie Emerson.

The movie never happened. "I would not separate the children," said Josephine. "Each one was as precious as the other and they all needed my supervision." Apparently Georgia agreed, reportedly saying, "I don't want to go to Hollywood. I want to go back to Boston Light."

Cover of the novel Storm Child, *by Ruth Carmen.*

Georgia, the "Storm Child," was subsequently featured in an article in *Flair* magazine. The writer, Marshall Hahn, described Georgia as a "sweet little powder-blue eyed blond" who had four dolls and a dog named Tinka. The article reported that the history of Boston Light was dramatized on a nationwide radio broadcast on NBC on August 7, 1939, featuring an interview with Keeper Maurice Babcock.

Georgia Norwood

The legend of the Storm Child lived on. Georgia's son, Willie Emerson, later wrote a book called *First Light,* which relates the true story of his mother's birth and life at Boston Light. Josephine told her grandson:

As we never knew when inspection of the houses, tower and fog signal would be held, it was a matter of course to have the beds made, the dishes done, and the sweeping and dry mopping done by ten o'clock. Of course our children were brought up to help with the work. Then they had their time to swim, go fishing, walking over the bar at low tide, or go rowing.

In November 1934, Betty Haskins, the pregnant wife of First Assistant Keeper Ted Haskins, had to be rushed by the Coast Guard to Hull during a northeast storm. The trip took twice as long as usual, but all went well.

Members of the Bostonian Society and the Massachusetts Historical Society held a ceremony on Little Brewster in December 1934 honoring the 25 keepers of Boston Light. Fitz-Henry Smith, author of a history of the lighthouse, unveiled a tablet bearing the names of the keepers. The modest and taciturn Maurice Babcock was invited to speak. Here is the entire text of his speech:

> *Well, ladies and gentlemen, I am not much of an orator, but I enjoy keeping the light burning for the ships coming in, and the fog signal sounding. I thank you.*

The historian Edward Rowe Snow, a resident of nearby Winthrop, was a frequent visitor to Boston Light during the Babcock era. He sometimes visited in the guise of the Flying Santa, a role he played for more than 40 years, bringing holiday season gifts in a show of appreciation for the region's lighthouse keepers and their families.

The unveiling of a plaque listing the station's keepers on December 2, 1934. Left to right: J. Lelan Hart, keeper from 1919 to 1926; Charles Jennings, keeper from 1916 to 1919; Maurice Babcock, keeper from 1926 to 1941, and Fitz-Henry Smith, author the 1911 book The Story of Boston Light. *From the collection of Edward Rowe Snow, courtesy of Dolly Bicknell.*

Most of the gifts were dropped from an airplane, but because oposal oposalhe lived nearby, Snow often brought the presents to Boston Light in person. In early January 1937, Snow directed an effort by the Youth League of Massachusetts, as they delivered around 40 bundles of food to Boston Light and the other lighthouses in the harbor.

Flying Santa plane passing Boston Light, 1947. Courtesy of Friends of Flying Santa.

Maurice Babcock was mentioned in newspapers in July 1938 after he had to sound the station's foghorn for 61 consecutive hours—a Boston Light record. Two month later, Babcock and his family were on the island for the devastating hurricane of September 21, 1938, which struck New England without warning. As the winds picked up late that afternoon, Keeper Babcock had to crawl on his hands and knees to reach the lighthouse.

A grandson of Keeper Maurice Babcock taking an outdoor bath on the pier at Little Brewster Island on July 31, 1940. Photo by F. F. Haskell, courtesy of Dolly Bicknell.

Babcock and one of his assistants spent the night in the lighthouse lantern, making sure the light stayed lit. A dock at the island was wrecked by the storm. Babcock's log entries, now at the National Archives, make note of the storm but mention nothing of his own extraordinary efforts.

Circa 1941 (U.S. Coast Guard)

In late 1939 Keeper Babcock lost part of a finger in an accident with a motor on the island. He spent a few weeks in Boston recuperating. In a newspaper article during that period, he said that he had never driven an automobile and had no intention of doing so. By boat he could reach Boston's South Station in 50 minutes, much faster than the trip by car from Hull.

"We do our shopping for groceries just as anybody else does," he told the reporter. "The only difference is that we are farther from the store. We lay in larger supplies than most people, on account of the distance. We can't trot out to the chain store if we happen to forget the coffee."

As mentioned previously, the young Benjamin Franklin composed a poem describing the death of Boston Light's first keeper, George Worthylake. Not a single copy of the poem was known to exist until 1940, when Maurice Babcock Jr., son of the keeper, found a tattered, yellowed copy in the pocket of a rotting leather jacket in the ruins of an old house on Middle Brewster Island.

Edward Rowe Snow helped young Maurice identify what he had found. The copy could not be proved to be authentic, so no value could be placed on it. The find was publicized in news media throughout the country. The narrative of the events surrounding the tragedy is fictionalized in Franklin's version (if this is Franklin's), with little resemblance to what really happened.

Maurice Babcock, photo by F. F. Haskell, courtesy of Dolly Bicknell

Edward Rowe Snow and Maurice Babcock in the 1930s, courtesy of Dolly Bicknell.

Maurice Babcock Jr. with the poem he found.

Here's the poem as printed on the copy found by Maurice Babcock Jr.:

The Lighthouse Tragedy

Oh! George. This wild November

We must not pass with you

For Ruth, our fragile daughter,

Its chilly gales will rue.

So, home to Lovell's Island

Take us when fails the sea

To the old house where comfort

And better shelter be.

Comes the long weary winter

With its storms of driving snow;

I can only watch the beacon

Sure that you are near its glow.

Yes, dear wife, my constant service

Binds me to this narrow isle,

Love must ever yield to duty

Though the heart be sad the while.

Only grant that on the morrow

We may safely pass the sea,

I can bravely bear my sorrow

You and Ruth here will not be.

With wild nor'wester came this morning,

Cold and clear the heartless sky.

Come wife, take Ruth. The pull will be long.

So - into the boat I will row you home.

Nestled within her mother's cloak

Frail Ruth is sheltered from the blast,

While Anne looks into George's face

With quick, strong strokes they leave the shore.

Though starting in the Brewster's lea,

Rough and empty rolls the sea.

Low the boat -- too deeply laden

Heavy hearts make heavy burden.

Now they reach the open channel

Where the flood tide breasts the gale

Rears a toppling wall of water.

Making Anne's cheeks grow pale.

Quick the prow is upward borne

George in Ann's arms is thrown

Husband, wife and child together

To the chilly waves have gone.

Frenzied clasp of wife and daughter

Bears the sturdy swimmer down,

Save the boat upon the water

Nothing of their fate is known.

Friends of the Babcocks threw the family a farewell party on the island on the day of the keeper's retirement in November 1941. Edward Rowe Snow accompanied Babcock on his final trip up the lighthouse stairs and later wrote:

It was a sad journey we made that afternoon, and as we reached the lantern room he looked fondly at the lenses and the lighting apparatus with its gas mantle, all of which he would never see again. Then Maurice Babcock, twenty-fifth keeper of Boston Light, stepped out on the platform that surrounds the tower and looked out to sea. Neither of us spoke, but each knew what was in the other's mind—the old days of the lighthouse service were gone forever, never to return.

Just after her husband's retirement, Babcock's wife told the *Boston Post:*

> *For 23 years we have been away from civilization. Now we'll join civilization again. And we are both glad and sorry. You don't surrender a 23-year routine without regret. But, all in all, we're glad to be back in the world again.*

Maurice Babcock, courtesy of John Babcock and Diana Cappiello.

6 THE COAST GUARD ERA

The U.S. Coast Guard took over the management of the nation's lighthouses in 1939, and civilian keepers were given the option of remaining civilians or joining the Coast Guard. After 12 years as an assistant to Maurice Babcock, Ralph Norwood enlisted in the Coast Guard and became the officer in charge in 1941.

Some of the Norwood clan on the fog cannon in the 1930s, courtesy of Willie Emerson.

In the 1930s and early 1940s there were many as 19 children

living on the tiny island. The school-aged Norwood children lived with their mother in Hull during the school year, but they always looked forward to their glorious summers on the island. "You never relaxed until they were all safely in bed at night," said Josephine Norwood. She once rigged a leash attached to the clothesline for her young son Bobbie, but "Georgia felt sorry for him and untied him."

Ralph Norwood's daughter Priscilla Reece later remembered that her father would go to Hull once a month for groceries. "Sometimes he would take one of us kids with him," she recalled, "and the grocers would feel sorry and give you a cabbage or something." Attempts to maintain a vegetable garden on the island met with little success, as the soil was poor.

The Norwoods, of course, always had plenty of seafood. The children would harvest the plentiful crabs, periwinkles, and mussels from the shores of the island. The older children made money by lobstering.

Summers were lively, filled with rowboat races and pie-eating contests with the children who summered on nearby Great Brewster. Games of all sorts were played, even baseball on Great Brewster—in the water was an automatic out. Life was generally harmonious, although Maurice Babcock Jr. once got a punch in the nose from one of the Norwood girls. He had trespassed onto the Norwoods' part of the island without permission.

When Norwood's daughter Fay (also known as Lila) Achor

died in Maine in late 2015, her friend Elaine Jones wrote in the *Boothbay Register* about the family's lighthouse years:

> *She said that making the climb with her father to "light-up" at night was a very special event. She loved seeing the beautiful beams of light exiting the lighthouse and was proud that her father was safeguarding the mariners from America's oldest lighthouse station.*
>
> *Each day, the children explored the intertidal zone, eager to discover what had washed ashore. One forbidden area to enter was a specific tide-pool with sea anemones that their father named "poison puddle." At a minus tide, a mussel bar allowed for passage to nearby Big Brewster Island, but they had to remain watchful of the incoming tide. Once, their dog Spunky went over to visit his girlfriend and got swept out to sea when attempting to swim home. Luckily, he was rescued by a fisherman and returned to them.*
>
> *Some of Lila's favorite childhood memories were associated with holidays. On the Fourth of July, the family consumed an entire watermelon while watching numerous firework displays along the Boston shoreline. The other was the annual airdrop of presents from the Flying Santa. Each year, the children waved to Santa (a.k.a. Edward Rowe Snow) as he flew over hoping that his package would miss the island yet remain retrievable to them. A failed drop would mean a second attempt and double the Christmas "goodies."*

Fay (Lila) Norwood Achor circa 1970s. Photo by Edward Rowe Snow, courtesy of Dolly Bicknell.

Ralph's son Bruce Norwood said years later, "I've never been in another place that felt like the home Boston Light was." The Norwoods left the island in 1945 and moved to Ram Island Light in Boothbay Harbor, Maine.

One of Ralph and Josephine's sons, Gail, later became a lightkeeper in Nova Scotia, making four generations of keepers in the family. Ralph C. Norwood died on Father's Day in 1987, at the age of 82.

Ralph Norwood inside the lens at Boston Light. Courtesy of Willie Emerson.

Boston Light was extinguished on September 8, 1942, for the remainder of World War II; it went back into operation in July 1945. The fog signal remained in operation during the blackout.

1945 photo by F. F. Haskell, courtesy of Dolly Bicknell

In September 1945 a brief article about the light station appeared in the Sunday *Boston* Globe. According to the writer, William H. Clark, the Coast Guard keepers sometimes looked longingly toward Boston. He quoted one: "We can at least dream we're in town, even if it seems forever before our six days' leave every month comes around again."

The light was converted to electricity in 1948, and shortly after that the clockwork mechanism that rotated the lens was replaced by an electric motor. The second-order Fresnel lens remains in use today.

Joseph E. Lavigne and family at Boston Light, early 1950s.

A baby boy was born on the island in March 1950 to Mary Ellen Lavigne, wife of Joseph E. Lavigne, the Coast Guard's principal keeper. When the baby's birth was imminent, low tide prevented the keeper from launching a boat to get his wife to the mainland.

A doctor was rushed over from Pemberton Point in Hull in a Coast Guard boat, and Joseph Jr. was delivered at 7:30 a.m. Mary

Ellen was later taken to Quincy City Hospital to recuperate. Joseph Jr. was the couple's first son and their fourth child.

In November 1952, a 22-year-old Coast Guardsman stationed at the lighthouse, Newton, Massachusetts, native Seaman Richard B. Fredey, traveled in one of the station's 14-foot boats to the Hull Yacht Club. The boat was powered by a five-horsepower outboard motor. With him was Wilford MacNeill, a 53-year-old civilian contractor who was doing work on the island.

Fredey and MacNeill were last seen in Hull around 3:30 a.m. on November 21. When they failed to return by later in the morning, an intensive search was conducted. MacNeill's body was later found, and Fredey was presumed dead. Fredey left his wife and a six-month-old daughter, and MacNeill left a wife and two children.

Richard Fredey and his daughter, Jill, at Boston Light. Courtesy of Jill Fredey Doering.

In 1960 it was decided that the smaller 1885 seven-room keeper's house would suffice for the island's Coast Guard personnel. The 1859 duplex dwelling had badly deteriorated. A 1949 inspection reported that the ceiling in the kitchen was falling down and there were rat holes in the house. The Coast Guard razed the structure in the spring of 1960. After that, Coast Guardsmen lived at the station without their families.

Boatswain's Mate First Class William "Mike" Mikelonis, a New Hampshire native, was the Coast Guard keeper at Boston Light for about five years beginning in 1962. The Coast Guard staff at that time spent two weeks on the island followed by one week off.

Mikelonis and other keepers over the years have enjoyed great fishing off the ledges. When Mikelonis retired in 1967, he said he had caught more than a thousand striped bass, two of them over 50 pounds. At his retirement party, Mikelonis was presented with the bulb that burned in the tower on his last day of duty.

Mikelonis shared the island with two assistants and a shaggy black dog named Salty, one of a long line of Boston Light dogs. Salty was succeeded by Salty II, and later by Farah (named during the era of *Charlie's Angels*), a friendly mutt who lived for 13 years on Little Brewster. Farah would whine and shake when taken to the mainland. Once, at low tide, Farah wandered over to Great Brewster Island, and 11 puppies resulted from her short trip away from home.

Farah died in November 1989, and her final resting place is a marked grave not far from the cistern building.

A later dog was named Shadwell in honor of the slave who drowned with the first keeper. Cats have also lived at the station, including a frisky black cat named Ida Lewis, after America's most famous woman lighthouse keeper.

A 1974 article in the *Christian Science Monitor* profiled Boatswain's Mate First Class Jim Turner, who claimed there was a "brisk pace" to life on Little Brewster. Each man on the crew at the time spent two weeks on the island followed by a week off. Turner's daily routine started early each morning with the dusting of the lighthouse lens, followed by much cleaning in the keeper's house and other buildings, then painting as needed.

Every three hours, Turner relayed weather data to the Coast Guard station at Point Allerton. On occasion, samples of the station's drinking water were sent to a lab for analysis. The lighthouse's powerful light was turned on each day exactly 15 minutes before sunset. If the visibility was bad, the foghorn had to be activated. To occupy the keepers in their off hours, the house was stocked with a TV, stereo, and a pool table.

The historic blizzard of February 6-7, 1978, forced the Coast Guard keepers to leave the house to take shelter in the base of the tower, on higher ground. The island was awash in the storm, which damaged the foundation of the house and did extensive damage to the pier.

Circa 1974 (U.S. Coast Guard).

The *Quincy Patriot Ledger* profiled the Coast Guard crew in the early 1980s. Two of the men—Pete Perron and Roger Emmons—had specifically requested to be assigned to the light station. "I've been interested in lighthouses since I was a little kid," said the 23-

year-old Emmons, who was from Florida. Lighthouse life could be lonely, he said, but he managed to keep busy with gardening and other activities.

Petty Officer Paul Dodds, who grew up in Hull with a view of Boston Light, became the officer in charge in early 1984. Dodds recalled sitting on a seawall as a boy, gazing at the lighthouse. By this time, Boston Light's fame as a National Historic Landmark (designated in 1966) was bringing more visitors to the island. Dodds was told that the island's historic significance was the only reason keepers were retained, instead of automating and destaffing the station.

During their stay, Dodds and Fireman Patrick Doherty painted the boathouse and converted the upper story into a gym, installed new doors, and supervised the installation of a new fuel line. The men split 12-hour watches.

Joe Larnard of Newburyport, Massachusetts, was another of the Coast Guard's keepers in the 1980s. Profiled in *People* magazine, Larnard said the view of the city was tantalizing. "We know we're missing out," he said, "so we stop looking. It's like being in a ship at sea, only we're on a rock that doesn't roll."

Larnard also alluded to the often-told tales of hauntings on the island. "I used to think the ghost stories were true, " he said, "what with the wind and all."

Some people have reported weird happenings on Little Brewster over the years. Russell Anderson was a Coast Guard keeper in 1947. One day his 22-year-old wife, Mazie, was walking along the shore. She heard footsteps close behind her, but saw no one when she turned around.

That night as she tried to sleep, Mazie felt a presence in the room. Later she heard what she described as "horrible maniacal laughter" coming from the boathouse. On another night she heard the same sound coming from the fog signal house. This time a little girl's sobbing voice followed, calling "Shaaaadwell!" over and over.

Mazie Anderson later related this story in an article in the October 1998 edition of *Yankee* magazine. She said that on one occasion the fog signal engines started themselves and the light mysteriously went on by itself. Mazie saw an unfamiliar figure outlined against the lens. Soon she again heard the man's laughing voice and the girl's sobbing cries. It wasn't until years later that Mazie Anderson discovered that the name of the Boston Light slave who died along with the Worthylakes in 1718 was Shadwell—the name repeated by the little girl's voice.

Petty Officer First Class Dennis Dever, the Coast Guard officer in charge in the late 1980s, had a few odd experiences. In a 1989 interview, he spoke of his love for reading Edgar Allen Poe books during storms on the island. While working in the station's boathouse, he liked to have his radio tuned to a rock station. Often, with nobody else in the boathouse, the station would change itself to a classical station. Dever said he and other Coast Guard crew attributed events like this to "Old George"—Worthylake, that is.

One day Dever was in the kitchen of the keeper's house looking out the window at the tower, and he clearly saw a man in the lantern room. This was alarming, as the only other person on the island was his assistant in the next room. From a distance, it appeared that the figure at the top of the tower was wearing an old fashioned keeper's uniform. Dever rushed to the tower and went up the stairs, but he found the lantern room empty.

Reports of mysterious figures seen in the tower and in the keeper's house continue to the present day. A number of people have described the ghostly figure of a woman in a white nightgown at the top of the tower.

By 1989 the Coast Guard had automated almost every lighthouse in the United States and Boston Light was scheduled to be the last in this process. Harry Duvall, an automation expert for the Coast Guard, started preparation for the process but voiced misgivings. "Automation can't maintain the building," he told a *Boston Globe* reporter.

It looked like Dennis Dever, a Maine native and the officer in charge since 1988, would be the light's last keeper, and possibly the last lighthouse keeper to be employed by the federal government in the nation. Dever relished the honor. "When sailors crossed those open seas and saw the lighthouse, they knew they'd made it. The keepers kept that light going. That is what compels me," he told a reporter.

In addition to his regular duties, Dever kept busy by creating two scarecrows designed to keep gulls off the dock, planting flower and vegetable gardens, and designing a Boston Light T-shirt.

Local groups—including the Friends of the Boston Harbor Islands and the Boston Harbor Association—protested the change to Congress and the Coast Guard, fearing that an abandoned station would fall to ruin. With the help of Massachusetts Senator Edward M. Kennedy, the plans to destaff the station were changed.

In October 1989 it was announced that the Senate Appropriations Committee had put specific language in the Coast Guard budget that would compel the Coast Guard to "retain staffing at Boston Light during fiscal year 1990 and conduct a review of its ownership, maintenance, and staffing." The First District commander, Rear Adm. Richard I. Rybacki, commented, "It's worth a long look to see where we want to put the balance between preserving our heritage and making the best use of taxpayer dollars."

In 1990 Historic Boston and the Massachusetts Department of Environmental Management commissioned a stewardship plan and preservation guidelines for the station. As a result of the study, much work was done on the island in the 1990s, including replacing trim on the keeper's house and repainting all the buildings.

Little Brewster Island was hit hard by the "Perfect Storm" of October 1991 and a December storm in 1992. Extensive damage to the buildings was repaired, but the storms also exacerbated concerns over the erosion of parts of the island, especially at the east end near the lighthouse.

Dennis Dever, the Coast Guard keeper in the late 1980s.

U.S. Coast Guard photo, courtesy of Dennis Dever.

7 AUTOMATION AND BEYOND

According to a 1995 article by the Associated Press, the Coast Guard was spending about $13,000 annually for the upkeep of the Boston Light Station, plus the salaries of three Coast Guard keepers. The two Coast Guardsmen on the island at the time of the article, Wesley Pannett and Mark Clement, expressed great fondness for the assignment, but they also said they felt isolated from "real" Coast Guard jobs, such as search and rescue. The summers were easy, but island life could be bone chilling in winter.

Boston Light became the last lighthouse in the United States to be automated on April 16, 1998. After automation, the Coast Guard crew continued to perform all the other traditional keepers' duties, except for turning the light on at sunset and off at sunrise. The light currently operates 24 hours a day.

Sally Snowman and Jay Thomson, both Massachusetts natives, met during Coast Guard Auxiliary training in 1993. Once, when they were in a boat passing Boston Light, Sally remarked that she had always fantasized about getting married there. Jay immediately replied, "Let me know when you want to do it." A year later they decided to set the date.

On October 8, 1994, Jay and Sally went out to Little Brewster Island on a friend's 32-foot sailboat named *True Love*. The 22 guests arrived at the wedding on one sailboat and two powerboats. After the ceremony the tower was opened for guests to climb. "I think the tower tour was as much the highlight of the trip as the wedding," said Sally.

Coast Guard Auxiliary (volunteer) personnel have worked on the island since 1980. Just a month after their wedding, Sally Snowman and Jay Thomson went back to Little Brewster to do their first lighthouse duty as Auxiliarists. Researching Boston Light's past became a passionate pursuit. The book *Boston Light: A Historical Perspective,* published in 1999, was the culmination of five years of research by Sally and Jay.

Sally Snowman has also written a children's book called *Sammy the Boston Lighthouse Dog*. Sammy, a black Lab who lived on the island from 1997 to 2004, was another in the long line of memorable dogs at Little Brewster. The book is narrated by Samantha, Sammy's successor as "official" lighthouse dog.

The Auxiliary personnel at Boston Light are now referred to as watchstanders, and a program was established for their training in 2000. In September 2003 Sally Snowman was appointed as the new keeper of Boston Light—the first civilian keeper since 1941, and the first woman keeper in the lighthouse's long history. The active duty Coast Guard personnel who had been assigned to the island were relocated to meet the needs of Homeland Security.

Sally Snowman, U.S. Postal Service photo by Daniel Afzal in 2013.

National Park rangers are also present during the days the island is open from June to October. The rangers are there during the day only, whereas the Watchstander Program requires that participants stay overnight on the island for four- to seven-day stretches.

During renovations in the summer of 2014.

8 VISITING BOSTON LIGHT

You can see Boston Light distantly from the shores of Hull, Revere, and Winthrop. The lighthouse can also be seen from sightseeing cruises out of Boston, including some of those offered by the Friends of the Boston Harbor Islands (see www.fbhi.org).

The Boston Harbor Alliance runs trips from Boston to Little Brewster Island in season. Visitors on these trips get to climb the 76 stairs to the top of Boston Light for a breathtaking view of Boston Harbor.

If you visit Little Brewster be sure to look on the rocks for initials and names carved by keepers and visitors to Boston Light, some dating back to the 1700s.

Visit www.bostonharborislands.org for details on how to visit Boston Light..

THE KEEPERS

George Worthylake (1716-1718)

Robert Saunders (1718)

John Hayes (1718-1733)

Robert Ball (1733-1774)

William Minns (1774-1776)

Thomas Knox (1783-1811)

Jonathan Bruce (1811-1833)

David Tower (1833-1844)

Joshua Snow (1844)

Tobias Cook (1844-1849)

William Long (1849-1851)

Zebedee Small (1851-1853)

Hugh Douglass (1853-1856)

Moses Barrett (1856-1862)

Charles E. Blair (1862-1864)

Thomas Bates, Jr. (1864-1893)

Alfred Williams (1893)

Albert M. Horte (1893-1894)

Henry L. Pingree (1894-1909)

F. E. Tarr (1909-1910)

Levi B. Clark (1910-1911)

George Kezer (1911)

Mills Gunderson (1911-1916)

Charles H. Jennings (1916-1919)

James Lelan Hart (1919-1926)

Maurice Babcock (1926-1941)

U.S. COAST GUARD

Ralph C. Norwood, (1941-1945)

Franklin A. Goodwin (1945)

Julio DiFuria (1945-1946)

Eldon W. Beal (1946)

Leo F. Gracie (1946-1948)

Stanley Batt (1948)

Joseph F. Lavigne (1948-1950)

John D. Hall (1950)

Robert C. Merchant (1950-1951)

Clinton M. Davis (1951)

Ray O. Beard (1951-1952)

Robert A. Reedy (1952)

John Curran (1952-1953)

Paul B. Guy (1953-1954)

Hubert B. Jones (1954-1955)

John E. Horner (1955-1959)

J. B. Collins (1959-1960)

Gottfried Schiffers (1960-1962)

William F. Mikelonis (1962-1967)

Vernon T. Springer (1967-1969)

Allick Rust (1969-1971)

Dennis I. Reed (1971-1972)

Edward J. O'Shea (1972-1973)

James H. Clark, Jr. (1973-1974)

James H. Turner (1974-1975)

Alan D. Achorn (1975-1977)

Carlton F. Brietzke (1977-1978)

Marvin D. Gonzalaus (1978-1980)

H. L. Murra (1980-1982)

James F. Burt (1982-1984)

Paul V. Dodds (1984-1985)

Guy A. Veillette (1985-1987)

Joe B. Lanard (1987)

K. J. Galvin (1987-1988)

Dennis Dever (1988-1990)

Alexander ("Sandy") Booth (1990-1992)

Wesley J. Pannett (1992-1995)

Reid Hair (1995-1997)

Scott Stanton (1997-1999)

Richard Himelrick (1999-2001)

Pedro Gonzales (2001-2003)

Sally Snowman (2003-)

Assistant keepers:

Sylvester F. Douglas (1854-?); Joseph Hammond (1856); Charles Hooper (1856-1857); Joseph Wonson (first asst., 1859-1862); J W. Wonson (second asst., 1859-1862); Walter Hooper (second asst., 1861-1862); Marcellus A. Blair (second asst., 1862); Charles E. Blair (first asst., 1862); Charles H. Barrett (second asst., 1862-1863); Wallace D. Hooper (first asst., 1862-1865); Peter Harrington (second asst., 1863-?); John C. Connell (1863-1866); Robert Shore (1863-1866); William Hooper (1865); Lyman Ford (1865); Joshua L. Bates (1865-1870); N. H. Woodbury (1866-1867); Alexander Tolman (1867-?); John Sheehan (1868); George A. Ordway (1868); William H. Sylvester (1868-1869); Walter Colby (second asst., 1869-1870); Daniel McKenzie (1870-1872); Fred Hammond (first asst., 1872-1877); David Keating (second asst., 1875-1876); George G. Baily (second asst., 1876-1877, first asst., 1877-1882); John Philbrook (second asst., 1877-?); E. Lewis Gorham (second asst., 1877-1878); William H. Hammond (second asst., 1878-1880); Edward L. Gorham (second asst., 1880-1882, first asst., 1882-1884); Alfred Gorham (second asst., 1882); Frank L. Carson (second asst., 1882-1884, first asst., 1884); Charles E. Turner (second asst., 1884-1886, first asst., 1886-1888); Henry L. Pingree (second asst., 1886-1888, first asst., 1888-1892); William Garvin (second asst., 1888); James P. Smith (second asst., 1888-1891); George G. Baily (second asst., 1891-1892); Albert M. Horte (second asst., 1892); Alfred Williams (first asst., 1892-1893); William A. D. Hadley (second asst., 1893); Gershom C. Freeman (second asst., 1893-1895, first asst., 1895); Wesley A. Pingree (first asst., 1894-1895); Daniel D. L. Donovan (second asst., 1895, first asst., 1895); Charles F. Stranger [Stanger ?] (second asst., 1895-1896, first asst., 1896); William A. Pool (second asst., 1895-1896, first asst., 1896-1899); Joseph

Keller (second asst., 1896-1899, first asst., 1899-1902); Ernest R. Sylvester (second asst., 1900-?); George E. Kezer (first asst., 1901-1905); Daniel E. Harding (first asst., c. 1901); Levi B. Clark (second asst., 1902-1904, first asst., 1904-1905); Charles W. Jordan (second asst., 1904-1905); Henry C. Towle (second asst., 1905-1907); William H. Oliver (second asst., 1907-1908, first asst., 1908); Joseph Philip Sousa (second asst., 1908, first asst., 1908-1910); Andrew S. Nickerson (second asst., 1908, first asst., 1911-1913); Charles H. Jennings (first asst., 1909-1911); ? Huse (second asst., 1913); ? McLaughlin (second asst., 1915); Martin Rolland (second asst., 1915); William G. Burtt (second asst., 1911-1912); William G. Mailbette (second asst., 1912); ? Kerr (second asst., 1913); Carl Delano Hill (asst., c. 1915-1916); James Lelan Hart (1916-1919); Charles Lyman (1916-1919); Ralph C. Norwood (second asst. 1929-1937, first asst. 1937-1941); William J. Howard (first asst., 1921-1923); Arthur Small (c.1917-1926); William Lane (first asst., 1927); Archford Vernon "Ted" Haskins (first asst., 1927-1937); J. E. Poyner (second asst., c. 1927); Frank J. Ponte (second asst., c. 1927); Osborne Earle Hallett (second asst., 1937-1943); Leo W. Wertman, Jr. (Coast Guard, second asst., 1950); James L. Cook (Coast Guard, second asst., 1951); Edward R. Benway (Coast Guard, second asst., 1951-1952); Leon G. Lewis (Coast Guard, first asst., 1952); Edward Whitmore (Coast Guard, first asst., c. 1952); Richard B. Fredey (Coast Guard, second asst., 1952); John G. Steen (Coast Guard, first asst., 1958); William G. Desautels (Coast Guard, second asst., 1958); Norman J. Kauffer (Coast Guard, second asst., 1958); Judson E. Boardman (Coast Guard, first asst., 1960); Donald M. Nashawath (Coast Guard, 1962-1967); David L. Vitale (Coast Guard, 1967-1969); Alan Letto (Coast Guard, 1967-1969); Bert Glazier (Coast Guard, 1969-1971); Norman Gannon (Coast Guard, 1969-1971); Peter Perron (Coast Guard, c. early 1980s); Roger Emmons (Coast Guard, c. early 1980s); Tony Kuliak (Kulik?) (Coast Guard, c. early 1980s); Robert

N. Greeley (Coast Guard, 1983-1984); Michael Bennett (Coast Guard, 1983); Patrick Doherty (Coast Guard, c. 1984); C. F. Ingham (Coast Guard, c. 1985); Joseph Allairi (Coast Guard, c. 1980s); ? Finnogan (Coast Guard, c. 1980s); Steve Stark (Coast Guard, 1986-1987); ? Danbby [Danby ?] (Coast Guard, 1986); Don White (Coast Guard, 1987); Tom Corcoran (Coast Guard, c. 1980s); David D. Sandrelli (Coast Guard, (1988-?); Kevin King (Coast Guard, c. 1988); ? Berg (Coast Guard, 1988); L. E. Wilkinson (Coast Guard, 1988); Jeffrey Currier (Coast Guard, 1988); Alan W. Ux (Coast Guard, 1989); James E. McClurkin (Coast Guard, 1989); Charles Joseph Pulaski (Coast Guard, 1990); ? Rosenburg (Coast Guard, c. 1992-1995); ? Wheeler (Coast Guard, c. 1992-1995); Mark Clements (Coast Guard, 1991-1995); Sean McGerry (Coast Guard, 1995-1997); Matt Fendley (Coast Guard, 1996-1997); Kevin Staples (Coast Guard, 1997-1998); Jeremy Rohanna (Coast Guard, 1997-1999); Chris Southerland (Coast Guard, 1998-1999); Gary Fleming (Coast Guard, 1999); Kevin Cullen (Coast Guard, 1999), William Cavanaugh (Coast Guard, c. 2000)

SELECTED BIBLIOGRAPHY

Anderson, Mazie B. "The Ghost of Boston Light." *Yankee*, October 1998.

Arias, Ron. "Turn Out the Lighthouse, the Party's Over; Keeper Joe Larnard Stoically Awaits Automation." *People*, circa 1980s; exact date unknown.

Arizona Republic, "World's Loneliest Light Switcher." December 25, 1994.

Aschenbach, Joy. "Lighthouse Closures Spell End of Long Tradition." *Blade-Citizen*, September 25, 1989.

Boston Gazette, March 24, 1735.

Boston Globe, "Lightkeeper Bates Dead." April 7, 1893.

Boston Globe, "Oldest Beacon on Coast Is Boston." July 31, 1904.

Boston Globe, "Angry Sea Cheated." May 21, 1906.

Boston Globe, "Happy School Days at Boston Light." October 2, 1910.

Boston Globe, "Boston Light to Have its First Flag Tuesday." June 9, 1917.

Boston Globe, "First American Flag to be Hoisted at Boston Light." June 27, 1917.

Boston Globe, "Tablet Ceremony at Boston Light." December 3, 1934.

Boston Globe, "Boston Light Keeper Almost a Commuter." December 8, 1939.

Boston Globe, "Finds Ballad by Franklin." August 7, 1940.

Boston Globe, "Last Resident Boston Light Keeper Retires Today, C.G. Taking Over." November 29, 1941.

Boston Globe, "Light housekeeping in Boston Harbor." September 9, 1945.

Boston Post, "Baby Boy Born at Boston Light." 1950; exact date unknown.

Boston Transcript, "The First Lighthouse in the United States." August 26, 1880.

Boston Traveler, "Battle Gale to Beat Stork to Lighthouse." April 1, 1932.

Benedict, Tobey. "One Manned Lighthouse Holds On." *Christian Science Monitor*, August 22, 1989.

Boston News Letter, November 24, 1718.

Boston Post Boy, June 5, 1754.

Caldwell, Bill. "'Storm Child' Outlives Fame in Boothbay." *Portland (ME) Press Herald*, December 2, 1986.

Caldwell, Gail. "To the Lighthouse." *Boston Globe*, August 26, 1984.

Candage, G. F. "Boston Light and the Brewsters." *New England*

Magazine, October 1895.

Carmen, Ruth. *Storm Child.* Bridgeport, CT: Braunworth, 1937.

Clark, E. S., Jr. "The First Lighthouse in the United States." *U.S. Naval Institute Proceedings* 63, no. 4, Whole no. 410 (April 1937).

Clark, William H. "Light Housekeeping in Boston Harbor." *Boston Globe*, September 9, 1945.

Clough, Samuel. *New England Almanac*. Boston, 1701.

Crittenden, Jules. "It's a Wonderful Dog's Life." *Boston Herald*, June 25, 1995.

Daly, Christopher B. "Keeping the Faith at America's Last Manned Lighthouse." *Washington Post*, December 25, 1991.

D'Entremont, Jeremy. "Josephine Norwood: First Lady of Boston Light." *Lighthouse Digest*, September 2003.

D'Entremont, Jeremy. *The Lighthouses of Massachusetts*. Beverly, MA: Commonwealth Editions, 2007.

D'Entremont, Jeremy. "Sally Snowman's Lighthouse 'Soul Work.'" *Lighthouse Digest*, May 2002.

DeWire, Elinor. *Guardians of the Lights: The Men and Women of the U.S. Lighthouse Servic*e. Sarasota, Florida: Pineapple Press, 1995.

De Wire, Elinor. "Keeping Boston Light." *Mariners Weather Log*, Summer 1991.

De Wire, Elinor. "A Point of Light." *Navy Times*, March 9, 1992.

Dixon, David, and Associates and Nancy Lurie Salzman. *Boston Light: Preservation Guidelines and Stewardship Plans*. Boston: Historic Boston Incorporated and Massachusetts Department of Environmental Management, 1990.

Emerson, Willie. *First Light: Reminiscences of Storm Child and Growing Up on a Lighthouse*. East Boothbay, ME: Post Scripts, 1986.

Galluzzo, John J. "Hull Has Always Claimed Lighthouse Kids for Her Own." *Hull Times*, March 26, 1998.

Gleason, Sarah C. *Kindly Lights: A History of the Lighthouses of Southern New England.* Boston: Beacon Press, 1991.

Gray, H.A. "Old Boston Light comes out of the shadows." *Boston Evening Transcript*, January 13, 1941.

Grossfeld, Stan. "With a View Like This, Why Go Anywhere?" *Boston Globe*, December 27, 1998.

Hartford, Philip. "A Woman's Life 23 Years on a Lighthouse." *Boston Post*, November 30, 1941.

Jennings, Harold B. *A Lighthouse Family*. Orleans, MA: Lower Cape Publishing Company, 1989.

Johnson, David. "Lighthouse Excursion Savors Harbor's Majesty." *South Look*, May 31/June 1, 1995.

Jones, Elaine. "Memories of Lila Fay Achor." *Boothbay Register*, December 14, 2015.

Kennedy, Dana. "Lighthouse Change Signals End of an Era." *Boston*

Herald, October 8, 1989.

Massachusetts Magazine, February 1789.

New England Weekly Journal, May 23, 1735.

New York Times, "Fog Problems Studied by Weather Scientists." December 4, 1927.

New York Times, "Franklin's First Writing Found after 175 Years." August 8, 1940.

Portland Press-Herald. "Lighthouse-born 'Storm Child' comes back to sea." April 9, 1971.

Power, J. H. "Boston Light's 200 Years." *Boston Transcript*, September 6, 1916.

Putnam, George R. *Lighthouses and Lightships of the United States.* Boston: Houghton Mifflin Company, 1933.

Shurtleff, Nathaniel Bradstreet. *A Topographical and Historical Description of Boston.* Boston: City of Boston, 1871.

Smith, Fitz-Henry. *Storms and Shipwrecks in Boston Bay*. Boston, privately printed 1918.

Smith, Fitz-Henry. *The Story of Boston Light*. Boston: Privately printed, 1911.

Snow, Edward Rowe. *The Islands of Boston Harbor.* Andover, MA: The Andover Press, 1935.

Snow, Edward Rowe. "Keepers of Boston Light." *Quincy Patriot Ledger*, April 22, 1967.

Snow, Edward Rowe. *The Lighthouses of New England*. New York:

Dodd, Mead & Company, 1973.

Snow, Edward Rowe. "The Maritime Benjamin Franklin." *Brockton Enterprise*, August 9, 1955.

Snowman, Sally, and James G. Thomson. *Boston Light: A Historical Perspective*. Plymouth, MA: Snowman Learning Center, 1999.

Snowman, Sally. " *Sammy the Boston Lighthouse Dog."* Privately printed, 2006.

Soundings, March 1995. "Last Manned Lighthouse is Boston's Loneliest Spot."

Storer, W. Scott. "The Guiding Light of Boston Harbor." *New England Galaxy*, Spring 1977.

U.S. Bureau of Light-Houses. *Two-Hundredth Anniversary of Boston Light*. Washington, D.C.: Government Printing Office, 1916.

Wheeler, Wayne. "America's First Lighthouse: Boston Light." *Keeper's Log*, Fall 1984.

Wilson, Robert E. "Old Boston Light." *Worcester Telegram*, September 5, 1965.

ABOUT THE AUTHOR

Jeremy D'Entremont is the author of fifteen books and hundreds of articles on lighthouses and maritime history. He is founder of Friends of Portsmouth Harbor Lighthouses, webmaster of www.newenglandlighthouses.net, and owner of New England Lighthouse Tours (www.newenglandlighthousetours.com).

He lives in Portsmouth, New Hampshire, with his wife, Charlotte Raczkowski, and their tuxedo cat, Evie.

At Boston Light, circa 1990.

Made in the USA
Lexington, KY
29 October 2016